In the Backyard

Sabrina Crewe

Consultant:
Professor Anne K. Camper,
Montana State University

CHELSEA CLUBHOUSE
An Imprint of Chelsea House Publishers

Chelsea Clubhouse
An imprint of Chelsea House
132 West 31st Street
New York NY 10001

Library of Congress Cataloging-in-Publication Data

Crewe, Sabrina.
  Under the microscope : in the backyard / Sabrina Crewe.
    p. cm. -- (Under the microscope)
  Includes index.
  ISBN 978-1-60413-822-1
  1. Microorganisms--Juvenile literature. 2. Microscopy--Juvenile literature. 3. Natural history--Juvenile literature. I. Title. II. Series.

  QR57.C74 2010
  579--dc22

                              2009039339

Chelsea Clubhouse books are available at special discounts when purchased in bulk quantities for businesses, associations, institutions, or sales promotions. Please call our Special Sales Department in New York at (212) 967-8800 or (800) 322-8755.

You can find Chelsea Clubhouse on the World Wide Web at http://www.chelseahouse.com

Text design by Sabine Beaupré
Illustrations by Stefan Chabluk
Originated by Discovery Books
Composition by Discovery Books
Cover printed by Bang Printing, Brainerd, MN
Book printed and bound by Bang Printing, Brainerd, MN
Date printed: May 2010
Printed in the United States of America

10 9 8 7 6 5 4 3 2 1

This book is printed on acid-free paper.

All links and Web addresses were checked and verified to be correct at the time of publication. Because of the dynamic nature of the Web, some addresses and links may have changed since publication and may no longer be valid.

Acknowledgments
We would like to thank the following for permission to reproduce photographs: Dennis Kunkel Microscopy, Inc.: pp. 5 inset, 8, 10, 14, 15, 17 left, 23, 25 bottom; Nijboer: p. 16; Sarefo: p. 18; Science Photo Library: pp. 6 (John Runions), 12 (Jeremy Burgess), 13 (Sinclair Stammers), 16 (Kenneth H. Thomas), 19 bottom (Andrew Syred), 20 (Jeremy Burgess), 25 top (Eric Grave), 29 (Andrew Syred); Shutterstock Images: pp. 4 (Elena Elisseeva), 5 main image (Andrey Pavlov), 11 left (Jubal Harshaw), 11 right (Brykaylo Yuriy), 17 right (Paul Cowan), 19 top (Damian Herde), 22 (Jens Stolt), 24 (Jubal Harshaw), 27 (Stephen Bonk); Martin Smith: p. 9.

Contents

Some words are **bold** the first time they appear in the text. These words are explained in the glossary at the back of this book.

The Invisible Backyard

Imagine a typical backyard—it has grass, flowers, and maybe a tree. It looks fairly peaceful out there.

Now take a closer look. You'll see insects moving around. Those bugs are the giants of the backyard! If you looked at the backyard through a microscope, you would see a whole new world of living things much tinier than those insects.

Microscopic life

Living things you need a microscope to see are called **microorganisms**. Microorganisms that aren't animals are often called **microbes**.

We share our world with many **microanimals** and microbes. Our large world depends on the microscopic

Micro-Fact

In a handful of backyard soil, there are billions of microorganisms! The dirt holds so many thousands of microscopic **species** that many don't even have names.

world because microorganisms play an important part in Earth's natural processes. The backyard is a great place to learn about the processes taking place in the soil under our feet.

Looking up close

Microscopes can reveal other things that are usually invisible to us. All living things are made up of tiny parts called **cells**. Before we meet the microbes, we are going to take a close-up look at cells and other microscopic parts in plants.

Animals that look small to us are huge compared to some micro-organisms. In real life, the ants below are only about 0.25 inches (6 millimeters) long. But they are thousands of times bigger than these **bacteria** (right), which also live in the backyard.

Plant Cells

Cells are the pieces that plants and animals are made of. They are the building blocks of living things. Your body, for example, has billions of different kinds of cells, each with its own function.

Plant cells also come in different shapes and sizes, depending on what their jobs are. But all the plant cells we can look at under the microscope have the same basic parts. These parts are known as **organelles**.

Cell wall

A plant cell has a wall that supports the cell and gives it a shape. The cell wall is formed of cellulose, which is a substance made from sugars. The cellulose protects the parts inside the cell. Inside the cell wall is another protective layer called the membrane.

Cell headquarters

Every cell has a **nucleus**. The nucleus acts as the headquarters for the cell. It directs activities, such as growth and reproduction.

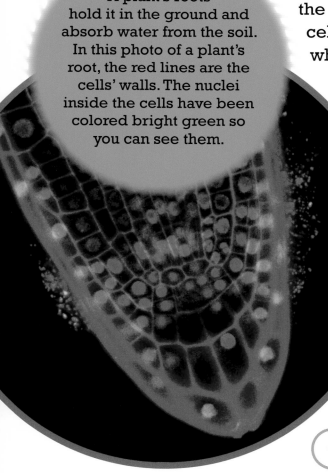

A plant's roots hold it in the ground and absorb water from the soil. In this photo of a plant's root, the red lines are the cells' walls. The nuclei inside the cells have been colored bright green so you can see them.

Other organelles

The cell's vacuole takes up much of the space in a cell. This is because it acts as the cell's storehouse. Vacuoles store **nutrients** and process waste. They also hold the water that keeps plants firm. When plants don't get enough water, the vacuoles shrink and the plant gets floppy.

The **chloroplast** you see in the diagram below is a very important organelle in plants. It produces chlorophyll, which gives plants their green color. We'll find out next how the tiny chloroplast makes food for plants and other living things.

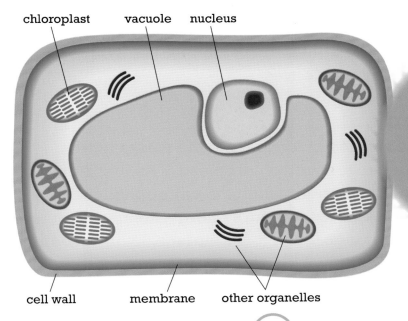

chloroplast   vacuole   nucleus

cell wall   membrane   other organelles

If we opened up a plant cell and put it under a very powerful microscope, these are the parts we would see inside.

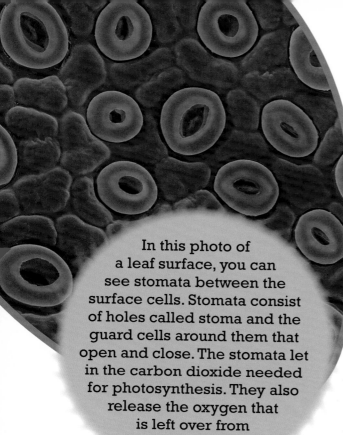

In this photo of a leaf surface, you can see stomata between the surface cells. Stomata consist of holes called stoma and the guard cells around them that open and close. The stomata let in the carbon dioxide needed for photosynthesis. They also release the oxygen that is left over from the process.

Inside the Leaf

The chloroplast is just one small part of one tiny plant cell. And yet it is amazingly important. Chloroplasts are the microscopic factories where plants make the food they need to grow. Only under a microscope can we see how this happens.

Photosynthesis

The process that chloroplasts use to make food is called **photosynthesis**. *Photo* means light, and *synthesis* means combining, or bringing separate things together. The light part is sunlight. The synthesis takes place in a plant's leaves.

The ingredients

Just below the surface of the leaf are the mesophyll cells. They are packed with chloroplasts. The first step in photosynthesis happens when the chlorophyll inside the chloroplast captures the sun's energy. Meanwhile, the stomata, tiny openings in the leaf's surface, let in carbon dioxide. And the leaf's veins deliver water from the plant's roots.

Food factory

Inside the chloroplast, these ingredients are combined. The Sun's energy allows the chloroplast to mix the carbon from the carbon dioxide with the hydrogen from the water to make food. This food is glucose, which is a kind of sugar.

One ingredient is left over: oxygen. The plant releases the leftover oxygen into the air. Most living things need oxygen, so that's a very useful job that plants do!

How Small Is Small?

A chloroplast is less than 10 **micrometers** across. (There are 1,000 micrometers in a millimeter and 25,400 micrometers in 1 inch.)

You can see the chloroplasts inside these plant cells because of their green color.

Energy for Everything

The glucose that plants make is essential for almost all other living things. People and other animals can't make their own food the way plants do. But we can get energy from eating plants or from eating other animals that eat plants. This transfer of energy makes plants, animals, and every other living thing part of an energy network that we call the food web.

Flowers and Pollen

Flowers in the backyard look beautiful without a microscope. When we magnify them, however, we discover tiny parts that are usually invisible.

Pollen

If you look between the petals of a flower, you will see slender stalks called stamens. The anther at the top of the stamen produces pollen. Pollen looks like powder until you put it under the microscope. Then you can see all the different pollen shapes that plants produce.

Some pollen is shaped to help the wind carry it a long distance. Other types of pollen, for example the spiky pollen in this photo, is designed to stick easily to visiting insects.

Traveling through the air

The job of pollen is to **pollinate** plants of its own species. To reach other plants, pollen has to travel to them. Some types of pollen have tiny wings that enable them to be carried by the wind. Others use insects to travel. When bees, butterflies, flies, and other insects visit flowers, their bodies get covered in pollen. The insects then visit other flowers, carrying the pollen with them.

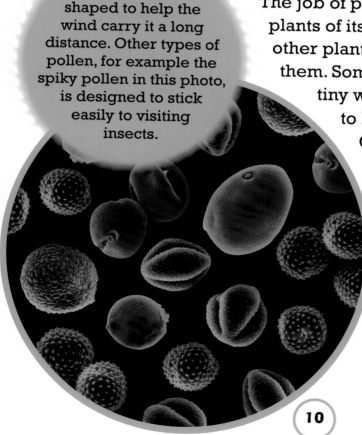

Pollination

Once pollen reaches another plant, it can start the process of reproduction. Pollen from one flower can pollinate another flower by **fertilizing** its eggs. The eggs turn into seeds, which will grow into new plants.

A new plant is growing inside these seeds.

Petal Virus

Flower petals are colored and scented to attract insects. But the colorful stripes in some tulips are not there for that reason—they are caused by a **virus** invading and damaging the cells. Viruses are the smallest microbes we know of. Many scientists say that they are not even a living thing, but more like a package of chemicals. Viruses can only multiply inside a living host, such as the cell of a plant.

Life in the Soil

The soil in which plants live and grow is also important to other living things. It provides a home for animals and microorganisms. In return, these living things keep soil healthy.

What is soil?

Soil is formed from many substances. It contains rock particles of different sizes, which we call sand, silt, and clay. Another ingredient is **organic** matter, or the remains of plants and animals. Soil also contains water and oxygen. And it is teeming with microscopic life!

How Small Is Small?

The threads of **microfungi** are so thin that a handful of soil can contain several miles of them!

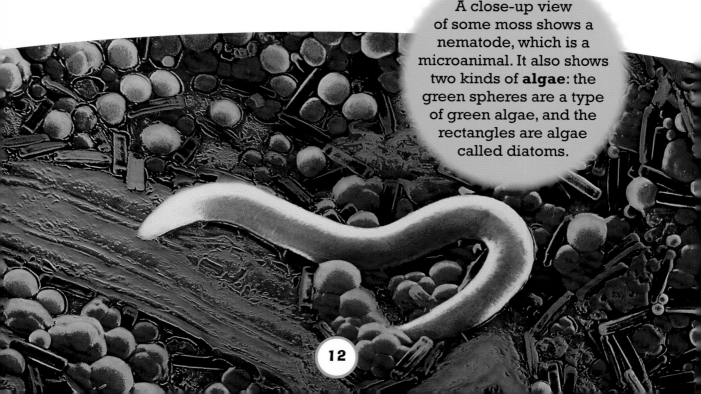

A close-up view of some moss shows a nematode, which is a microanimal. It also shows two kinds of **algae**: the green spheres are a type of green algae, and the rectangles are algae called diatoms.

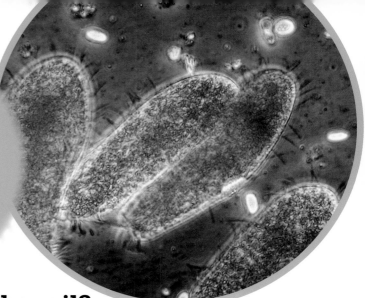

Ciliates are protozoa. They get their name from the cilla, which are the tiny hairs they use to move around and catch food with. These ciliates are living in a drop of water within the soil.

What's living in the soil?

There are so many kinds of microorganisms that we can't name them all. But we can divide them into basic groups:

- Microanimals have more than one cell and can digest food. They have a fixed body shape.
- **Protists** usually have one cell, but a few have more cells. Protists called algae are like plants, while **protozoa** are more like animals. Most protists live in water.
- Microfungi can also have a single cell or many cells. They form networks of **hyphae** through the soil and elsewhere. They reproduce with **spores**.
- Bacteria have a single cell with no nucleus. Many live on other living things, such as animals, or on decaying matter. They are much smaller than animals, plants, protists, and **fungi**.
- Viruses are more a package of chemicals than a real **organism**. They are even smaller than bacteria. A virus needs a host in order to multiply.

Let's take a closer look at some of these microorganisms.

Bacteria

Bacteria are everywhere in the backyard. There are so many different kinds that scientists haven't identified them all. Each bacterium has only one cell, but bacteria often live clumped together in colonies, or groups.

How Small Is Small?

You could fit more than 1,000 bacteria on the period at the end of this sentence.

Shapes and sizes

Bacteria come in a range of sizes, but they are almost all too small to see without a microscope. And like other living things, bacteria have many different shapes. There are, however, three basic forms that most bacteria take: spheres, rods, and spirals.

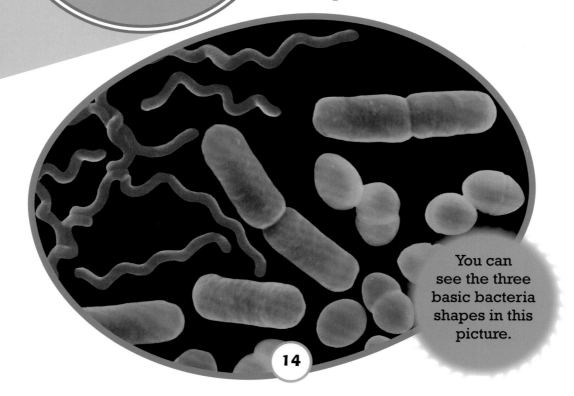

You can see the three basic bacteria shapes in this picture.

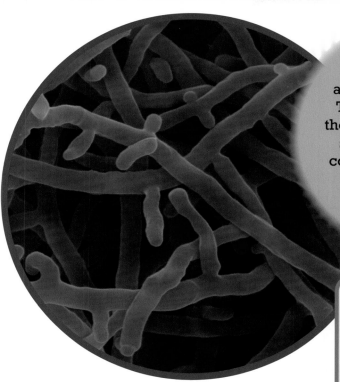

Soil gets its earthy smell from actinomycetes bacteria. They form threads, like the hyphae of fungi, which spread through soil or compost. They can break down tough stuff such as woody stems and tree bark.

Dividing and multiplying

Bacteria reproduce constantly by dividing themselves. In the right conditions, some bacteria can divide three times in an hour. So, as you can imagine, there are billions of bacteria around us.

Useful bacteria

Bacteria have many useful jobs to do in the backyard. Most bacteria are **decomposers**, turning dead matter into nutrients. Other bacteria help to break down polluting substances. Some fight diseases that harm plants.

Making Compost

Turn over a pile of dead leaves from last fall, and you may find a black crumbly substance. This rotted matter is what gardeners make in their backyard compost piles. Of course, it's actually bacteria that are doing most of the work. The bacteria eat the remains, breaking them down into smaller pieces. While bacteria eat, they release nutrients that make soil healthy.

The cloud you can see coming out of this puffball mushroom consists of billions of microscopic spores. Only a few of them will become new fungi.

Fungi and Microfungi

Fungi come in all sizes, from giant mushrooms to microfungi. In the backyard, you can find several kinds.

Fungi live on the remains of plants and animals. As they consume these remains, they turn them into useful nutrients for other living things in the backyard soil.

A mass of threads

Big or small, most fungi get food through their hyphae. Together, hyphae form into a mass or web called a **mycelium**. A few kinds of fungi form partnerships with plants. They live on the plants' roots and get food from the plants. As the fungi grow and spread their hyphae threads through the soil, they gather nutrients, which the plants' roots absorb.

Spore explosion

Most fungi also produce fruiting bodies, which is what they use to reproduce. Fruiting bodies contain spores, which are like the seeds of new fungi. They burst out of the fruiting bodies to float on the air. If they land in the right place—on a source of food—they will grow into new fungi.

Mildew

Several types of microfungi cause mildew to appear on backyard plants. To our eyes, mildew looks like a powder spread over a leaf. Up close, you can see its hyphae and spores. Mildews eat into leaves and flowers, which damages the plant.

These purple threads are powdery mildew on the surface of a leaf.

Yeasts

Yeasts are microfungi that have only one cell and no spores. If you have fruit growing in your yard, you might see a dusty coating on it. This coating is made from yeast cells. Because they have no spores, yeast cells reproduce simply by producing another cell called a bud.

Microanimals

You probably know that animals come in all shapes and sizes. Fish, insects, and birds are all animals. We know this because they have the cells of animals and because they feed and reproduce a certain way. Some of the microscopic creatures we find in the backyard soil are small animals, with animal cells like those of a whale or a dog. They just happen to be very tiny!

Along with bacteria and fungi, many microanimals work as decomposers to keep soil healthy. They also hunt other creatures, so they help with pest control in the backyard.

Micro-Monster

Pseudoscorpions are microscopic bugs that look like real scorpions but are actually similar to spiders. Like scorpions, they have pincers to catch other micro-organisms. Then they inject poison that paralyzes their **prey**. Pseudoscorpions often travel by riding on larger animals—you can see one on the leg of this fly.

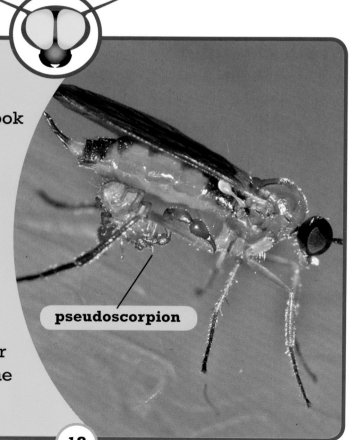

pseudoscorpion

Nematodes

Apart from bacteria, one of the most common life-forms you could find in the backyard are nematodes. They are useful as well as plentiful. Nematodes destroy backyard pests and release nutrients for plants.

Tardigrades and tuns

If you looked into a damp area, such as some moss or lichen, you might find some tardigrades. You would need a microscope to see them because they are less than 1 millimeter long. Also known as water bears, these funny little animals need water or they dry out. If they do dry out, however, they don't die. They curl up into a little wrinkly ball, called a tun, and become inactive. Once they have water around them again, they recover and carry on as usual.

If you pick up a teaspoon of soil, you are probably holding hundreds of nematodes like this one. Backyard soil is full of these microanimals.

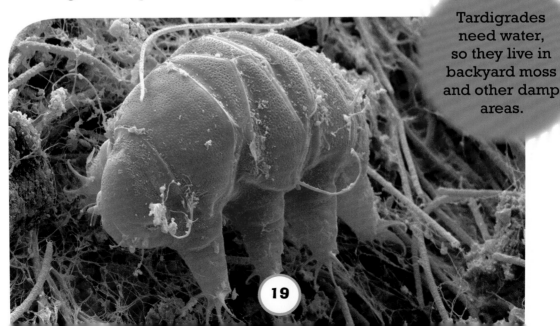

Tardigrades need water, so they live in backyard moss and other damp areas.

Recyclers and Fixers

Let's take a look at how all the microorganisms we've seen work together as part of an ecosystem.

Living together

An ecosystem is the name we give to a community of living things and its environment. The living part of the ecosystem includes animals, plants, fungi, and bacteria. The environment is the soil, water, light, and air they live in. Plants and animals in all ecosystems depend on each other to survive.

Depending on the microworld

The tiniest organisms are often the most important part of the ecosystem. This is because they are recyclers. Rotting remains are delicious food to some fungi and many bacteria. They recycle dead things and used things, turning them into valuable substances for other organisms, such as plants, and even you!

Other microbes take the gas nitrogen from the air. They process it so other organisms can use it. You can learn about this process in the panel opposite.

This is a rhizobium bacterium attached to the root of a plant. It converts nitrogen from the air into nitrates that plants can use.

Nitrogen Providers

As decomposers process their food, they release nitrogen from the remains into the soil.

Nitrogen is a valuable nutrient. Animals and plants need nitrogen to survive. But even though it is everywhere in the air around us, most living things can't absorb nitrogen from the air. This is where the microworld can help.

Microbes called nitrifying bacteria and nitrogen fixers can turn nitrogen into nitrates. This is a form of nitrogen that plants can absorb. It is passed onto animals when they eat the plants. So you can see that without microbes, we wouldn't get the nitrogen we need to exist!

There is another group of bacteria that can release nitrates from the soil back into the air. All these processes together create a cycle that moves nitrogen between soil, air, plants, and animals.

You can see how microbes fix and release nitrogen in this diagram.

Nitrogen gas is in the air all around us.

Animals get nitrates from plants.

Plants absorb nitrates through their roots.

Decomposers (bacteria and fungi) release nitrogen from plant and animal remains. Then nitrifying bacteria turn the nitrogen into nitrates.

Denitrifying bacteria release nitrogen gas into the air.

Nitrogen-fixing bacteria in soil and on plant roots turn nitrogen into nitrates.

Insects Up Close

Did you know there are 200 million insects for every one person in the world? The backyard is teeming with them, so let's look at some insects up close.

Horrible heads

Something really fantastic to look at under the microscope is the eye of an insect, such as a fly or mosquito. Instead of having one lens in each eye, like people do, insects have eyes made up of many lenses. You can see a pair of these eyes in the panel opposite.

Insects have some other strange-looking parts on their heads, too. Some have antennae covered in tiny hairs that pick up signals. Mosquitoes feed through a proboscis, a long tube they use to suck blood from people and animals.

Beautiful patterns

Butterflies are insects with beautiful patterns on their wings. When you look at the wings under a microscope, you can see that the patterns and colors are made from thousands of tiny scales.

A close-up look at this butterfly wing shows the scales that give the wing its patterns.

Micro-Monster

The magnified head of this male blackfly looks like something from a science fiction movie. Its compound eyes are made up of thousands of lenses. You can see there are two sizes of lens, with the larger lenses at the top. Two antennae are sticking up in front of the fly's eyes. Below are the mouthparts, with which the fly sucks up nectar from flowers.

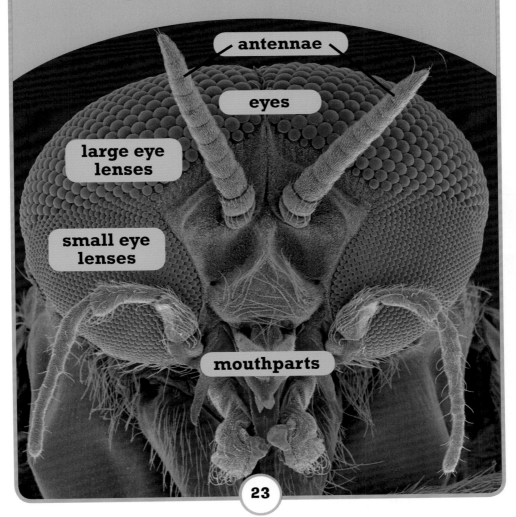

antennae

eyes

large eye lenses

small eye lenses

mouthparts

In a Water Puddle

There is always some form of water in the backyard, whether it's in a fountain, a birdbath, in the soil, or just a puddle. You'll be amazed at the microscopic world within a puddle of water!

Protists

A single drop of water contains many life-forms. Microscopic plants, animals, and bacteria live in water, just as they do on land. In the puddle, you will also find protists. As we learned earlier, protists are microorganisms that can behave like plants or animals. One kind of protist found in backyard water is a diatom. Diatoms are plant-like protists, or algae. They use photosynthesis to make food and grow. Unlike plants, however, diatoms have only one cell.

Diatoms come in all kinds of shapes, and they are really beautiful under the microscope.

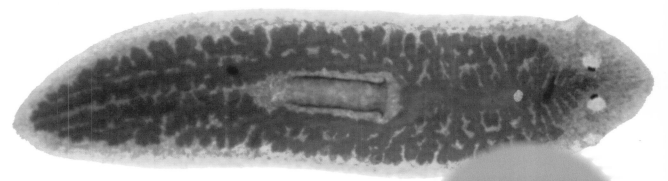

Planaria

Planaria are tiny worms that live in water. They glide around eating even tinier things, such as bacteria and protists. Some are as long as 20 millimeters, so you might see one in the backyard.

Planaria hide under debris or rocks in water because they don't like light. Their light sensors give them a distinctive cross-eyed look.

Mosquitoes

Many of the microscopic animals in water are a young form of bigger creatures. Mosquitoes, for example, live in water during the early stages of their lives. Adult female mosquitoes lay their eggs in any still water they can find, such as a puddle or backyard rain barrel. In this photo you can see a young mosquito, or **larva**, hatching from its egg. The larva will live in the water until it is ready to become an adult. Then it will live on and near water.

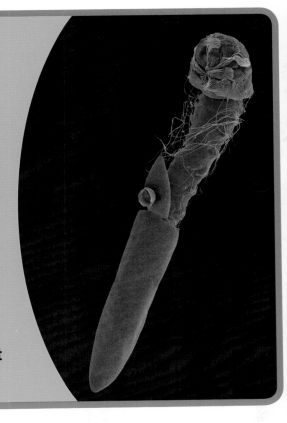

The larvae of bark beetles ate the tissues in this elm tree, leaving feeding tracks in its trunk.

Above the Ground

Let's take a look at the microscopic world in the trees and other plants we see in many backyards.

Life in the trees

Just as we found in the soil and water, there are many microorganisms living in trees and on other plants. Each tree may host hundreds of bacteria species as well as all kinds of fungi, plants, and animals. Some of these are good for plants, but others are harmful.

Tree attack

Bark beetles are tiny, but they can cause a lot of damage to even the biggest trees. They chew through the bark to get to the wood inside.

One kind of bark beetle helped spread a disease by carrying microfungi from one tree to another. The microfungus infected elm trees all over the world with

Dutch elm disease. This tiny fungus killed millions of trees in North America.

Bugs feeding on bugs

A **parasite** is a creature that lives in or on another living thing. Parasitic wasps are tiny, only about 3 millimeters long. They lay their eggs on aphids, caterpillars, and other pests that eat plants. When the eggs hatch, the wasp larvae feed on their host and kill it.

Micro-Monster

Gall mites are tiny insects in the arachnid family (like spiders) that like to munch on leaves. As the mites munch, the leaves grow around them, forming little lumps called galls. If you look in the backyard, you might see galls on the leaves of trees or smaller plants.

A parasitic wasp laid its eggs on this caterpillar.

Size and Scale

In this book, we measure some things in millimeters and even smaller measurements. This is because inches are just too big for measuring microorganisms and microscopic parts of things. Millimeters are pretty small, and micrometers and **nanometers** are so tiny that they are impossible to see with the naked eye and hard to imagine. There are more than 25 million nanometers in just one inch!

1 inch =	**25.4 millimeters**
1 millimeter =	**1,000 micrometers or 1,000,000 nanometers**
1 micrometer =	**1,000 nanometers**

Only the smallest of microbes are measured in nanometers. Some of these, such as viruses, have to be magnified hundreds of thousands of times before we can see them. Other microorganisms are huge compared to viruses, but we still need to magnify them to see them clearly.

About Microscopes

Many of the images you have looked at were produced using an electron microscope. Electron microscopes can magnify things many thousands of times, so they are used to magnify viruses, bacteria, and tiny parts of cells.

At home or in school, we use optical microscopes. They usually magnify things anywhere between 20 and 1,000 times, depending on the lenses you are using. It's always fun to take an everyday object, like a hair from your head or a leaf from the yard, and look at it under the microscope. Some of the images we have seen are made by optical microscopes with cameras attached.

Wake up a Tun!

It's not hard to find tardigrades in the backyard. They live in moss on trees, walls, and plant pots. You can probably find tardigrades in their tun stage in a piece of dried moss. Collect some moss and put it under the microscope to see if you can identify a tun. Tuns are wrinkly and about 0.3 millimeters in length. If you find one, add a few drops of water. (Distilled water is best because it doesn't have any chemicals that might harm the tardigrades.) Keep watching to see what happens. After a while, you should see the tun's legs and head reappear, and it should start moving around.

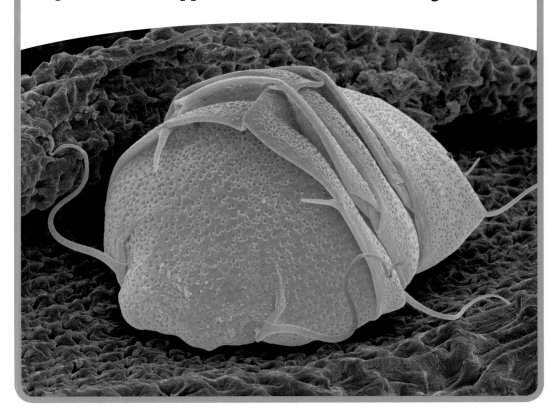

algae—protists that are similar to plants

bacteria—microorganisms with only one cell that are the smallest and most numerous life-forms on Earth

cell—tiny unit that all livings things are made of

chloroplast—organelle in a plant cell that is responsible for making chlorophyll and producing food through photosynthesis

decomposer—life-form (including bacteria, fungi, and animals) that breaks down remains of other living things

fertilize—start the process of reproduction

fungi—organisms similar to plants but with no ability to make food, so they live on other organisms (living or dead).

hyphae—threads that most fungi use to grow and spread through their food source

larva—stage of an insect after it has hatched from an egg but is not yet an adult.

microanimal—tiny bug or other animal too small to be seen clearly without a microscope

microbe—microorganism that is not a microanimal. Microbes also include viruses even though they are not really organisms.

microfungi—fungi that are microscopic or are made up mostly of microscopic parts

micrometer—measurement of length that is one-thousandth of a millimeter

microorganism—any living thing that is too small to be seen properly without a microscope

mycelium—network of hyphae

nanometer—measurement of length that is one-millionth of a millimeter

nucleus—part of a cell that controls the cell's form and functions

nutrient—substance that is a building block for living things and helps them grow and stay healthy

organelle—various parts inside a cell, each of which has its own function

organic—coming from a living thing, such as compost, which is made from decomposed plant matter

organism—any living thing, such as a plant, animal, or bacterium

parasite—organism that lives on or in another living thing and feeds off it

photosynthesis—process by which plants and algae use sunlight to combine carbon dioxide with water and make food

pollinate—transfer pollen from one flower to another to fertilize it

prey—living thing hunted or caught by another for food

protist—usually single-celled microorganism that lives in water or damp places. Protists can be plantlike (algae) or animal-like (protozoa).

protozoa—protists that are similar to animals

species—group of living things of the same kind. Bears, for example, are a kind of animal, but grizzly bears are a species.

spore—reproductive part of a fungus

virus—microbe that can only multiply by infecting living cells

Explore These Web Sites

Cells Alive! Cell Models
http://www.cellsalive.com/cells/3dcell.htm
Take an interactive look at plant cells and other cells.

Marly Cain's Microscopy for Kids
http://www.rmcain.com/mcama/adv/advidxkids.mv
Find all kinds of microscopic projects.

Kids' Valley Garden—A Gardening Resource for Kids
http://www.copper-tree.ca/garden/compost.html
Learn how to make your own compost pile.

Index